IMAGES
of America

HARNETT
COUNTY

THE SMOKESTACK AT ERWIN MILLS.

IMAGES
of America

HARNETT
COUNTY

John Hairr

ARCADIA

Published by Arcadia Publishing,
an imprint of Tempus Publishing, Inc.
2 Cumberland Street
Charleston, SC 29401

Printed in Great Britain.

Library of Congress Catalog Card Number: 98-86582

For all general information contact Arcadia Publishing at:
Telephone 843-853-2070
Fax 843-853-0044
E-Mail arcadia@charleston.net

For customer service and orders:
Toll-Free 1-888-313-BOOK

Visit us on the internet at http://www.arcadiaimages.com

*Dedicated to
the people of Harnett County*

Contents

CONFEDERATE VETERANS. This turn-of-the-century photograph shows a group of Confederate veterans gathered at the Chicora Cemetery on the Averasboro Battlefield. (Photograph courtesy of Sion Harrington III.)

Introduction

Harnett County was created by an act of the North Carolina Legislature on February 8, 1855. Prior to that time, the new county had been the northern part of Cumberland County, which was created in 1754. Before 1754, all of Cumberland had been contained in Bladen County, which stretched west to the Mississippi.

Harnett has a long and colorful past dating back to the early 1700s, when European settlers first arrived in the Cape Fear Valley. Many Highland Scots settled along the Cape Fear River and points west. Among their chief neighbors were Englishmen, Ulster-Scots, Welshmen, Frenchmen, and a few Germans.

Harnett County is located near the geographical center of the state, and lies between the two metropolitan areas of Fayetteville and Raleigh. The land is diverse, with the northwestern portion occupying a part of the Piedmont and the southeastern part of the county lying with the Atlantic coastal plain. Meanwhile, the southwestern portion of the county is part of the Sandhills physiographic region. The highest points in Harnett are part of the Sandhills and reach nearly 500 feet in elevation. The most prominent and influential physical feature in Harnett is the Cape Fear River, which bisects the county into almost equal halves. In fact, when legislation was being debated to create the county back in 1855, the region nearly received the name Cape Fear County. The Cape Fear River is the largest river contained entirely within the state of North Carolina. The river begins at the junction of Deep and Haw Rivers at Mermaid's Point, 7 miles upstream from Harnett's northwestern border. The river tumbles across the fall line as it flows through Harnett, giving the river a uniquely rugged character not seen elsewhere along its course.

Throughout its history, Harnett has been a predominantly rural county inhabited by small farmers and middle-class artisans who have produced just about every kind of crop grown in the South. Cotton has long been an important crop in the county. Shortly after the turn of the twentieth century, tobacco was introduced, and it has played a vital role in the lives of many Harnett citizens ever since. One agricultural commodity which was once an integral part of life in Harnett was the production of naval stores—tar, pitch, and turpentine. This lively business disappeared prior to World War I with the destruction of the longleaf pine ecosystem on which the industry depended. Vast stretches of Harnett were once covered with great forests of longleaf pines, but they are only a memory now.

Despite being a rural county, Harnett has also played host to much industry. Iron ore was once extracted and manufactured into steel at the famous Buckhorn Iron Works in the northwestern part of the county. The most important industry, however, was the manufacture of denim. Erwin Mills in Erwin is the largest denim factory in the world, and since its creation has been the largest civilian employer in the county.

With such a diverse background, chronicling the history of Harnett is a monumental task well beyond the scope of this work. This book is but a glimpse into our rich and honored past, and will hopefully serve to inspire others to delve deeper into the history of Harnett County.

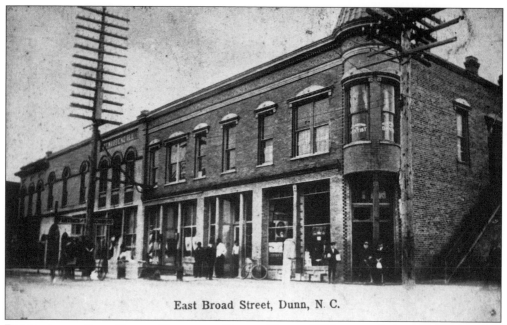

East Broad Street, Dunn, N. C.

POSTCARD OF EAST BROAD STREET IN DUNN. This *c.* 1900 postcard shows people milling about a street corner on Broad Street.

LUCKNOW COTTON YARD, DUNN, N.C.

THE LUCKNOW COTTON YARD IN DUNN. It was a busy center of commercial activity in the early part of the twentieth century.

One

People, Places, and Things

Despite its natural resources, international industries, and other high honors, Harnett's most valuable resource is its people. The people who settled and developed Harnett County were a tough and industrious lot. The fact that they were able to maintain their identity and stave off becoming a faceless suburb, despite being squeezed between the big cities of Raleigh and Fayetteville, is a testimony to their individualism and resilience.

Collected in this section are random shots of the everyday things which had an impact upon the lives of early residents. A few pictures of schools, churches, and events which defy categorization have also found a place in this section of the book.

THE CAM ROB STRICKLAND FAMILY. Here, members of the family stand in front of their home near Averasboro in 1898.

DUNN PROGRESSIVE INSTITUTE, BUILT IN 1888.

STORE OF W.H. GREGORY, 1905. This store stood in the old business district of Angier before it was destroyed by fire.

THE HISTORIC WILLIAMS GROVE SCHOOL. Now the focal point of a park in Angier, the old school remains a prominent landmark today.

W.H. Gregory's Store in Angier, 1905.

Angier Methodist Church, as It Appeared in 1905.

OLD ANGIER TEACHERAGE. Built c. 1930, the teacherage stood across from Angier School.

ANGIER SCHOOL (POSTCARD).

HORSE ON THE ROOF! The horse adds an interesting twist to this scene of downtown Angier in 1920.

HARVEY STEPHENSON HOME IN ANGIER, 1930.

DRUGSTORE BUILDING IN DOWNTOWN ANGIER, C. 1930.

DEPOT STREET IN ANGIER, C. 1950.

15

Angier Methodist Church Building, Constructed in 1936. The structure was destroyed by fire in 1985.

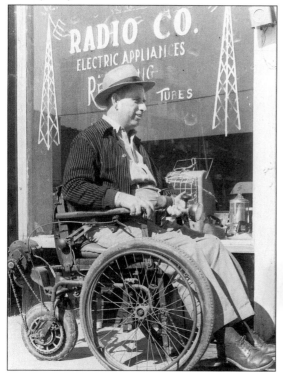

Mr. Lester Woodall of Angier, with an Early Model Electric-Powered Wheelchair. (Courtesy N.C. Department of Archives and History.)

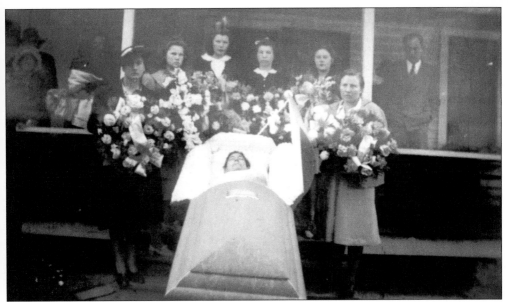

WAKE IN ERWIN, C. 1930. In the early 1900s and before, wakes were often held in the home of the deceased.

FAMILY GATHERING, 1945. Reunions such as this one were a common part of the social life for Harnett residents.

MALCOLM FOWLER, ERWIN NATIVE AND NOTED HISTORIAN OF THE CAPE FEAR VALLEY.
Fowler published two books, *They Passed This Way* and *Valley of the Scots*. He also wrote numerous newspaper and magazine articles, and was a frequent contributor to Carl Goerch's the *State* in the early days of that popular publication. Mr. Fowler was a co-founder and past president of the North Carolina Society of State and Local Historians (now the North Carolina Society of Historians). Each year, this group gives an award in Malcolm's honor to a historical society that has distinguished itself in the preservation and perpetuation of history.

MALCOLM FOWLER AND FRIEND.
Besides being steeped in the past,
Malcolm was a noted electronics
expert. Here he is repairing a
television with his friend
Alexander McArtan (seated).

LEON MACDONALD. Mr. MacDonald
was a local historian who was well
versed in the lore and traditions of the
Scots who settled the Sandhills of
western Harnett.

Paul Green, Harnett's Most Famous Playwright. Green is best remembered for his outdoor drama, *The Lost Colony*. He won a Pulitzer Prize for his play *In Abraham's Bosom* in 1927.

FLOODING, 1945. Water reaches window height on Watkins Garage north of Lillington during the 1945 floods of the Cape Fear.

DUNN HIGH SCHOOL'S FRESHMAN CLASS OF 1928.

Left: **FINAL RESTING PLACE.** This is the burial site of the stranger who froze to death on the steps of Barbecue Church on a cold winter's night in 1766.

Right: **SUMMERVILLE GRAVE.** Like Barbecue Church, Summerville also has a "stranger" buried in its graveyard.

"CAIRN OF REMEMBRANCE,"
ERECTED ON THE ORIGINAL SITE
OF BARBECUE CHURCH.

PAINTING OF THE FAMED SCOTTISH HEROINE FLORA MacDONALD. MacDonald is said to have attended services at Barbecue Presbyterian Church, and this painting by Eleanor Abbot recreates one of those visits. (Courtesy Presbyterian Historical Society.)

STUDENTS AT PARKER'S GROVE SCHOOL, c. 1913. The school operated in what is now a private home beside Erwin's Chapel Church, across the road from Cape Fear Christian Academy.

STUDENTS AT DUKE SCHOOL, 1924.

RAVEN ROCK, 1957. Here, Christine Smith stands beside ice formations at Raven Rock.

BOBBY SMITH, WITH AN EARLY MODEL METAL DETECTOR NEAR RAVEN ROCK IN 1958.

DRY SEASON. In 1954, this area experienced such extreme drought that Cape Fear River nearly ran dry.

THE ATKINS LOW GROUNDS NEAR LILLINGTON DURING THE DROUGHT OF 1954.

CHARLIE GILCHRIST AND HIS WIFE, EDNA THOMAS HUNTER GILCHRIST. Note the Confederate Veteran medal Mr. Gilchrist is wearing.

CAPTAIN HENRY BARNES, COMPANY B, 10TH BATTALION, N.C. HEAVY ARTILLERY. Barnes, who lived near the present town of Coats, commanded the Black River Tigers during the War Between the States.

PICNIC NEAR COOL SPRINGS CHURCH, C. 1900.

GROUP PORTRAIT TAKEN OUTSIDE THE FIRST COOL SPRINGS CHURCH STRUCTURE.

THE SECOND COOL SPRINGS CHURCH BUILDING, RECONSTRUCTED IN 1924. The structure stood until it was replaced in 1957.

E.S. Freeman and Bobby Freeman beside Mr. Freeman's House near Mamers in 1937. The blocks were handmade by E.S. Freeman.

Five Generations of Gilchrists. John Gilchrist, Mae Gilchrist Patterson, Hilda Patterson (and daughter), and Edna Gilchrist were photographed near Cool Springs Church in 1936.

Jim and Mary Gilchrist with Cornelius Smith near Raven Rock, c. 1930.

Duncan Cameron's Store in the Boone Trail Community, c. 1940.

DOWNTOWN DUNN IN 1905.

DUNN HIGH SCHOOL'S ELEVENTH GRADE CLASS FOR THE SCHOOL YEAR 1930/31.

GROUP OF STUDENTS FROM DUNN HIGH SCHOOL, 1931. Students are pictured from left to right as follows: (bottom row) J.J. Goldstein, W. Purdie, J. Thornton, M. Tilghman, E. Jones, Ed Smith, and B. Baldwin; (middle row) Lloyd Wade, L.B. Pope, U.L. Aldridge, L. Dupree, E. Culbreth, and J. McLeod; (top row) H. McKay, M. Wade, W. Baggett, and S. Smith.

KIVETT BUILDING AT CAMPBELL UNIVERSITY. Kivett is the oldest building on campus.

CIRCUS PARADE. Multitudes turned out to watch the circus parade along Broad Street in Dunn on October 14, 1902. (Courtesy N.C. Department of Archives and History.)

BROAD STREET IN DUNN, 1899.

CAPE FEAR RIVER PICNIC, 1885. This unidentified group found a way to get everyone in the picture.

THE HOTEL LILLINGTON, ONCE A POPULAR LANDMARK IN LILLINGTON. (Courtesy N.C. Department of Archives and History.)

POSTCARD OF THE HOTEL LILLINGTON. (Courtesy N.C. Department of Archives and History.)

FIRE, MARCH 30, 1948. Many Lillington residents gathered to watch the Bill Salmon house on the corner of Ninth and Front Streets burn. (Courtesy Lillington Fire Department.)

GATHERING OUTSIDE THE OLD FIELD CHURCH, C. 1890.

PLEASANT MEMORY CHURCH, AS IT APPEARED IN 1952. (Courtesy N.C. Department of Archives and History.)

THE WILLIAM AVERA HOUSE, CONSTRUCTED C. 1829. This house was the birthplace of Malcolm Fowler. (Courtesy N.C. Department of Archives and History.)

COUNTRY STORE NEAR BUNNLEVEL.

TWO UNIDENTIFIED INDIVIDUALS BESIDE A STILL. This photograph was taken in western Harnett, c. 1940.

PLEASANT UNION SCHOOL, 1908. (Courtesy N.C. Department of Archives and History.)

HAPPY SOUNDS. This crowd gathered *c.* 1895 at the corner of Wilson Avenue and Broad Street to enjoy the sounds of the Who, What, When Minstrels.

A POPULAR PASTIME. Deer hunting has long been a popular pastime in the forests and sandhills of Harnett.

COLEMAN LUCAS IN FRONT OF HIS HOME NEAR DUKE, 1916.

SKETCH OF THE BATTLE OF AVERASBORO. This sketch appeared in *Harper's Weekly* in 1865.

SUMMERVILLE PRESBYTERIAN CHURCH. This house of worship has served the people of the Upper Cape Fear Valley since 1811.

THE CARLYLE WILLIAMS HOME NEAR LINDEN.

A PORTION OF THE OVERHILLS ESTATE AS IT LOOKED IN 1924. (Courtesy N.C. Department of Archives and History.)

STREET SCENE OF CITY MARKET AND TRIANGLE SERVICE STATION IN COATS, APRIL 29, 1948. (Courtesy N.C. Department of Archives and History.)

MARKER HONORING THE LOCAL MEN WHO FOUGHT IN THE BATTLE OF AVERASBORO.

Two

County Government and the Court House

The first meeting of Harnett County officials took place in Summerville Academy on March 11, 1855. There they named several government officials and established the workings of county government. A site for a county seat was soon thereafter chosen to include Summerville Academy. The new town was called Toomer.

Toomer remained the county seat until 1859, when the voters of Harnett voted to move the courthouse to Lillington, at that time nothing more than a wooded bluff overlooking the Cape Fear River. Despite several challenges throughout the years, Lillington has remained the county seat ever since.

The first county courthouse was built in Lillington in 1860/61. Unfortunately, there are no known photographs of this structure available at the present time (1998). This wooden building was destroyed by fire in October of 1892. The county seat used a couple of temporary buildings in Lillington for a courthouse until a new brick structure could be constructed in 1897/98. This building, though it has been the recipient of several renovations, still stands atop the picturesque bluff along the Cape Fear.

SUMMERVILLE ACADEMY. The first meeting of the county officials in Harnett County took place at Summerville Academy, which stood near Summerville Church.

GEORGE W. PEGRAM. Mr. Pegram, who lived near Cokesbury, was a prominent leader in old Cumberland and Harnett Counties. He represented Cumberland in the House of Commons from 1846 to 1852, and later represented Harnett in the State Senate from 1874 to 1875. He has the distinction of being the first county official elected in Harnett County in 1855, serving as chairman for the Court of Pleas and Quarter Sessions.

JAMES JOHNSON. Mr. Johnson was Harnett's first sheriff, and he lived near Buie's Creek.

CLERK OF THE COURT HOWARD GODWIN AND CHAIRMAN OF THE COUNTY COMMISSIONS ANGUS CAMERON. Here, they are standing inside the Harnett Court House in this World War II–era photograph.

Pen-and-Ink Sketch by Albert Harrell. This drawing depicts Harnett's only legal execution, which occurred in what is now the parking lot behind the courthouse in Lillington. The execution was quite a spectacle, drawing 6,000 spectators. Harrell was an eyewitness to the proceedings, which occurred on November 17, 1897, and afterwards he carried Ed Purvis's body to Dunn for Dr. Ollen Lee Denning. Dr. Denning dissected the body, reassembled the bones, and hung Purvis's skeleton in his office in Dunn. The office burned in 1927, but legend maintains that Purvis's bones were removed before the blaze and thus survive to the present day.

ED PURVIS. This is an artist's sketch taken from an old newspaper. Purvis was the only man to be legally executed in Harnett County.

"Ed Purvis is a mulatto, about 18 years of age, and says he has eight other brothers, says he has been tramping since he was nine years old." County Union, 15 September 1897

LAW ENFORCEMENT OFFICERS IN THE COURTHOUSE IN LILLINGTON, 1952. Pictured are Herman Word, Bill Grady, Wade Stewart, B. Leonard, and Kirkland Stewart. (Courtesy N.C. Department of Archives and History.)

WALTER BYRD. This prominent Lillington resident was photographed in 1921 at his desk in the Raleigh State Senate Offices. A prominent Republican leader, Byrd held many elected offices including county surveyor and clerk of the court, in addition to his term in the state senate.

HARNETT COUNTY COURTHOUSE, 1930. Notice the arrowhead-shaped Daniel Boone marker.

HARNETT COUNTY COURTHOUSE, 1956.

AN ADVERTISEMENT IN A 1959 EDITION OF THE *STATE* MAGAZINE. This ad shows an architect's conception of the courthouse renovations.

AN ADVERTISEMENT FROM THE 1950S EXTOLLING THE VIRTUES OF THE COUNTY SEAT.

Three

Transportation

Transportation has played a key role in the lives of Harnett citizens since the first days of settlement. In the earliest days, most folks preferred to travel on the rivers and streams of the region. Poll boats, canoes, and rafts carried goods and people deep into the interior of the state.

Native American trails became paths for the settlers, and these in turn were replaced with roads, turnpikes, and other thoroughfares to accommodate the travelers of each respective era. Railroads eventually entered the county to transport goods and people in a method much more reliable than the streams and dirt roads. The Fayetteville and Western Plank Road, a highway that stretched from Fayetteville to Betharbara, cut across the western edge of Harnett County in the 1850s. This was the longest wooden highway ever constructed, and is a popular topic of discussion among several historically minded individuals, especially in the Johnsonville area. Now, as the twentieth century draws to a close, airplanes and helicopters are a common scene in the skies over Harnett.

Log Railroad Trestle in Angier, 1937.

W.H. Gregory. Mr. Gregory posed for this picture in front of his home in Angier in 1905.

MILEPOST. This marker once stood alongside the Fayetteville and Western Plank Road in western Harnett County. The notches represent miles from the road's terminus in Fayetteville. The Fayetteville and Western has the distinction of being the longest wooden highway ever built. (Courtesy N.C. Department of Archives and History.)

BARCLAY'S INN AT BARCLAYSVILLE. This establishment was once a popular stopping place along the Stage Road. (Courtesy N.C. Department of Archives and History.)

"RING EAR" SAM JOHNSON'S INN IN JOHNSONVILLE. Constructed in 1854, this quaint inn accommodated travelers along the plank road. Johnson received his nickname because he wore rings in his ears like a pirate, which was quite a fashion statement in his day. (Courtesy N.C. Department of Archives and History.)

THE STAGE ROAD IN AVERASBORO. The Battle of Averasboro was fought along a stretch of the stage road south of Averasboro.

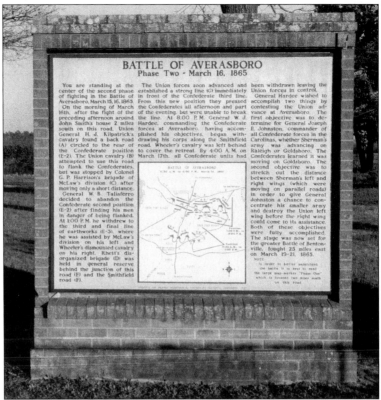

BATTLE OF AVERASBORO
Phase Two - March 16, 1865

You are standing at the center of the second phase of fighting in the Battle of Averasboro, March 15, 16, 1865.

On the morning of March 16th, after the fight of the preceding afternoon around John Smith's house 2 miles south on this road, Union General H. J. Kilpatrick's cavalry found a back road (A) circled to the rear of the Confederate position (E-2). The Union cavalry (B) attempted to use this road to flank the Confederates, but was stopped by Colonel G. P. Harrison's brigade of McLaw's division (C), after moving only a short distance.

General W. B. Taliaferro decided to abandon the Confederate second position (E-2) after finding his men in danger of being flanked. At 1:00 P.M. he withdrew to the third and final line of earthworks (E-3), where he was assisted by McLaw's division on his left and Wheeler's dismounted cavalry on his right. Rhett's disorganized brigade (D) was held in general reserve behind the junction of this road (F) and the Smithfield road (F).

The Union forces soon advanced and established a strong line (G) immediately in front of the Confederate third line. From this new position they pressed the Confederates all afternoon and part of the evening, but were unable to break the line. At 8:00 P.M. General W. J. Hardee, commanding the Confederate forces at Averasboro, having accomplished his objectives, began withdrawing his corps along the Smithfield road. Wheeler's cavalry was left behind to cover the retreat. By 4:00 A.M. on March 17th, all Confederate units had been withdrawn leaving the Union forces in control.

General Hardee wished to accomplish two things by contesting the Union advance at Averasboro. The first objective was to determine for General Joseph E. Johnston, commander of all Confederate forces in the Carolinas, whether Sherman's army was advancing on Raleigh or Goldsboro. The Confederates learned it was moving on Goldsboro. The second objective was to stretch out the distance between Sherman's left and right wings (which were moving on parallel roads) in order to give General Johnston a chance to concentrate his smaller army and destroy the Union left wing before the right wing could come to its assistance. Both of these objectives were fully accomplished. The stage was now set for the greater Battle of Bentonville, fought 25 miles east on March 19-21, 1865.

NOTE
In order to better understand the battle it is best to read the large map-marker "Phase One" which is located two miles south on this road.

CLASSIC CAR. Mr. John Williford shows off his automobile.

A Popular Mode of Transportation. Dolly Lucas is riding her mule in front of her family's home, *c.* 1920.

A. & W. RAILROAD SCHEDULE
Eastbound

No. 1 mixed leaves Sanford 8 a. m. arrives Lillington 9:27. No. 3 first class leaves Sanford 11:35 a. m., arrives Lillington 1:01 p. m. No. 5 first class leaves Sanford 5:50 p. m., arrives Lillington 7:16.

Westbound.

No. 2 first class leaves Lillington 8:20 a. m., arrives Sanford 9:46. No. 4 mixed leaves Lillington 11 a. m., arrives Sanford 12:45. No. 6 first class leaves Lillington 4 p. m., arrives Sanford 5:26.

Trains Nos. 2, 6, 3, 5 will be operated daily including Sunday. Trains Nos. 1 and 4 will be operated as mixed (second class) on Monday, Wednesday and Friday; as passenger (second class) on Tuesday, Thursday and Saturday. Trains Nos. 1 and 4 will not be operated on Sunday.

TRAIN SCHEDULE FOR THE ATLANTIC & WESTERN RAILROAD, 1920.

BOBBY FREEMAN. Bobby is sitting atop a 1939 Chevrolet near Mamers.

TURN-OF-THE-CENTURY PHOTO. A western Harnett resident posed for the camera with his bicycle.

THE CHATHAM. This locomotive saw service on the Western Railroad between Fayetteville and Egypt. This photograph was taken at the factory in 1866. (Courtesy N.C. Department of Archives and History.)

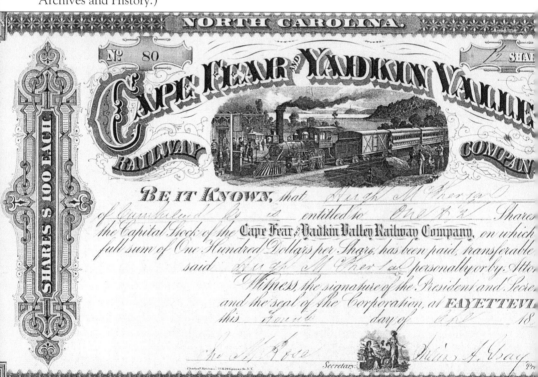

STOCK CERTIFICATE. In 1879, Hugh McPherson was issued this document for one and a half shares of stock in the Cape Fear and Yadkin Valley Railway, which took the place of the Western Railroad.

DOWNTOWN ANGIER, 1920. Notice the horse and buggy in the foreground.

JOHN MCARTAN AND FRIEND. These two men were photographed at the Rock Hill Service Station near Anderson Creek, *c.* 1950.

LOCAL EATERY. Ma's Kitchen was a popular stopping place for traffic on Highway 301 prior to the construction of I-95. The caption of this old postcard reads, "That famous Name and Place, Hwy. 301—3 miles South of Dunn, N. Carolina, 23 North of Fayetteville."

THE FIRST LOCOMOTIVE TO OPERATE ON THE CAPE FEAR AND NORTHERN RAILROAD. This railroad connected Apex and Dunn, and its name was later changed to Durham and Southern.

Early Autos. Many of the forest wardens drove their automobiles to a 1924 meeting on the Overhills Estate. (Courtesy N.C. Department of Archives and History.)

Norfolk & Southern Depot in Duncan, 1946. (Courtesy N.C. Department of Archives and History.)

UNIDENTIFIED WESTERN HARNETT FARMER WITH HIS MULE AND WAGON.

BUGGY RIDE. Two unidentified gentlemen enjoy a ride near Duke, *c.* 1910.

CROSSING AT CHALYBEATE SPRINGS. Highway officials inspect the railroad in 1921. (Courtesy N.C. Department of Archives and History.)

RAILROAD CROSSING ON THE ROAD INTO LILLINGTON, 1921. (Courtesy N.C. Department of Archives and History.)

HUSS, A FERRYMAN OF THE AVERASBORO FERRY, C. 1900. (Courtesy N.C. Department of Archives and History.)

DUNN BOYS WITH THEIR BIKES IN FRONT OF THE METHODIST CHURCH. From left to right, the individuals pictured are as follows: Paul Cooper, John Hodges, John Whithead, Rev. G.T. Adams, John Snipes, Joe Strickland, L.B. Pope, Edward Parker, David Dowd, and Marvin Wade.

A LOCOMOTIVE ON THE RALEIGH AND CAPE FEAR RAILWAY, 1903. This company operated the railway line connecting Raleigh and Fayetteville, which cuts through the center of Harnett County. The company later became part of the Norfolk Southern Railway.

A NOTICE PRINTED IN THE *HARNETT POST* ON SEPTEMBER 21, 1917. It outlines the schedule of arrivals and departures from Lillington.

Norfolk Southern

NORFOLK SOUTHERN OPER-ATES PASSENGER TRAINS FROM NORTH CAROLINA INTO TERMINAL STATION, NORFOLK, WITHOUT TRANSFER.

N. B. The following schedule figures published as information only and are not guaranteed.

Trains Leave Lililngton.

NORTHBOUND.

No. 32, 9:16 a. m. daily except Sunday for Raleigh and intermediate stations.

No. 34, 3:19 p. m. daily except Sunday for Raleigh and local points.

No. 86. 10:35 a. m.. Monday, Wednesday and Friday for Raleigh and local points.

No. 134, 3:07 p. m. Sunday only for Raleigh and local stations.

SOUTHBOUND.

No. 33 , 10:03 a. m. daily for Fayetteville.

No. 87. 12:40 p. m. Tuesday, Thursday and Saturday.

No. 35, 3:19 p. m. daily except Sunday for Fayetteville. Close connections at Raleigh to and from all points beyond.

For complete information apply to A. A. Todd. Ticket Agent, Lillington, N. C.

J. F. DALTON,
General Passenger Agent,
Department P.. Norfolk, Va.

THREE BUGGIES ON THE CAPE FEAR RIVER BRIDGE AT DUKE, SUMMER OF 1904. The first buggy is carrying James B. Duke; F.L. Fuller and Benjamin Duke are in the second buggy; and W.A. Erwin and T.J. Walker are in the third. (Courtesy N.C. Department of Archives and History.)

AN AIR SHOW. By the mid-twentieth century, airplanes were a common sight in Harnett. A good airshow such as Bo Bo Howard's Air Show in 1950 at the Erwin Airport could still draw a large crowd.

Four

Agriculture, Industry, and Commerce

Harnett County has been blessed with diverse resources by which the people have been able to make a living off the land for nearly three centuries. In the early days, the inhabitants were mainly subsistence farmers, concerned with producing the crops necessary for survival. It wasn't long before people started prospering in the fertile land, and soon people had the leisure to produce crops for food and money.

Until recent years, the majority of Harnett citizens relied on the products of the county's farms to make a living. This is even true of the county's largest industry, the production of denim. Erwin Mills was established in this region to both harness the natural power of Smiley's Falls and to take advantage of the large amount of cotton produced locally.

Forest resources have also played a big role in the lives of Harnett people. Just a couple of generations ago, there were many Harnett County citizens engaged in the massive naval stores industry. But the great longleaf pine forests were depleted less than a hundred years ago, and this industry died. Today, the forest industry is active in the county, taking logs for lumber mills and pulpwood.

DANIEL AND SARAH FAIRCLOTH. This couple typifies the small farmers who inhabited early, rural Harnett. Daniel was a Confederate veteran.

CAMERON'S HILL FIRETOWER, c. 1926. This firetower was the first tower the State of North Carolina constructed on private land.

"Here's to the land of the long leaf pine,
The Summer Land, where the sun doth shine,
Where the weak grow strong and the strong grow great,
Here's to Down Home, the Old North State."

22189

NAVAL STORES. The production of naval stores—tar, pitch, and turpentine—from the longleaf pine forests was an important part of Harnett's economy until World War I.

TOOL BOX OF HARNETT FIRE WARDEN J.A.D. MCCORMICK, 1925. A note on the back of this photograph indicates that the following items were stored in the shed: one knapsack, two torches, four waterbags, one saw, two axes, one hoe, two lanterns, two watering cans, five 2-gallon buckets, and three tools. (Courtesy N.C. Department of Archives and History.)

CANE MILL. Cane mills were a common feature across Harnett County prior to World War I.

ONE OF THE HOUSES AT EDEN COLONY, C. 1910. The village revolved around the production of dewberries, berries similar to blackberries.

MARVIN, ALICE, AND MEL BETHUNE. The Bethunes are shown grading cucumbers with the help of James McNeil, Gilbert McDougald, and Art McDougald.

HOG KILLING TIME. Hog killings were a common feature of farm life in Harnett County. This one was on the J.C. Byrd place near Bunnlevel, *c.* 1945.

LUCAS FARM HOG KILLING. This photograph was taken around the turn of the century near Old Field Church.

MR. HENRY TURLINGTON. Mr. Turlington (left), who lived between Erwin and Coats, was a U.S. marshall as well as a renowned hog farmer. (Courtesy N.C. Department of Archives and History.)

FARM WORK. Work on the cucumbers continued.

THE SORREL FAMILY ON THEIR
TURKEY FARM IN ANDERSON CREEK,
c. 1950. (Courtesy N.C. Department
of Archives and History.)

TOBACCO PLANTING. Mr. and Mrs.
John Callon planted tobacco the old-
fashioned way. (Courtesy N.C.
Department of Archives and History.)

COTTON WAITING BY THE TRACKS FOR SHIPMENT IN ANGIER, 1915.

DUNN'S FIRST ELECTRIC PLANT, C. 1900.

JOHN MCKAY'S MANUFACTURING COMPANY. McKay's company was a prominent landmark in Dunn when this photograph was taken in 1930. (Courtesy N.C. Department of Archives and History.)

FOUNDERS OF ERWIN MILLS. This group posed at Duke, North Carolina, at the time of the opening of the mill in the summer of 1904. The following are pictured from left to right: (seated) B.N. Duke, W. Duke, J.B. Duke, T.J. Walker, J.W. Goodson, unidentified, and J.E. Angier; (standing) Dr. A.G. Carr, W.A. Erwin, J.E. Stagg, Frank Tate, E.S. Yarborough, George Lemmon, and F.L. Fuller. This photograph was taken by R.H. Beasley of Goldsboro. (Courtesy N.C. Department of Archives and History.)

ROBERT "BUDDY" STRICKLAND, 1950. Mr. Strickland was photographed with his dog and cow on his farm near Erwin.

MILKING COWS. Milking was a common chore on farms throughout the region well into the mid-twentieth century. Shirley Strickland of Erwin is shown here milking the cow on her family's farm in 1950.

COWS. These animals were an important part of the agricultural economy of Harnett.

THE DUNN BRANCH OF THE FCX. This feedstore was a popular spot for farmers to purchase supplies. (Courtesy N.C. Department of Archives and History.)

JOHN WASHINGTON LUCAS AND HIS WIFE, SARAH FAIRCLOTH LUCAS, ON THEIR FARM NEAR ERWIN.

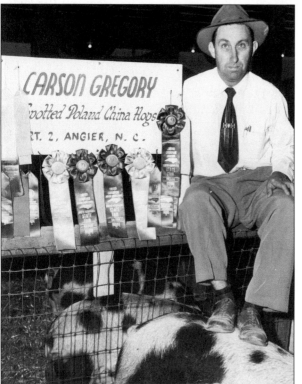

FARMER'S UNION. Thanks to the Populist movement of the late nineteenth century, small farmers began to get involved with their government and keep informed on the issues. The group of farmers shown here was gathered for a meeting of the Farmer's Union at Erwin's Chapel Church in 1905. (Courtesy N.C. Department of Archives and History.)

CARSON GREGORY OF ANGIER. He is shown here at the 1953 State Fair in Raleigh with numerous prizes for producing hogs. In addition to being a successful farmer, Gregory served the people of Harnett as their representative in the General Assembly.

Five

The Cartographic Record

In order to fully understand the development of Harnett County, it is necessary to explore some of the maps that have been produced throughout the years showing the area which now comprises Harnett. The earliest known map that shows a feature which can be identified as being in Harnett was drawn c. 1715 and showed the invasion routes of South Carolinians in their attacks during the Tuscarora War. Tuscarora Jack Barnwell crossed the Cape Fear at the mouth of Lower Little River and traversed the eastern portions of the county in 1711.

Since that time, many maps and charts have been produced of the Harnett area for a variety of reasons. River charts, railroad surveys, road maps, and town maps are all included here to give readers some idea of how the county has been perceived through the years, and how it has changed.

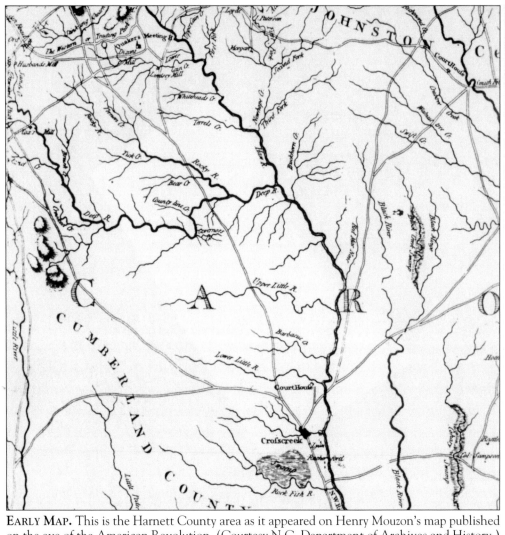

EARLY MAP. This is the Harnett County area as it appeared on Henry Mouzon's map published on the eve of the American Revolution. (Courtesy N.C. Department of Archives and History.)

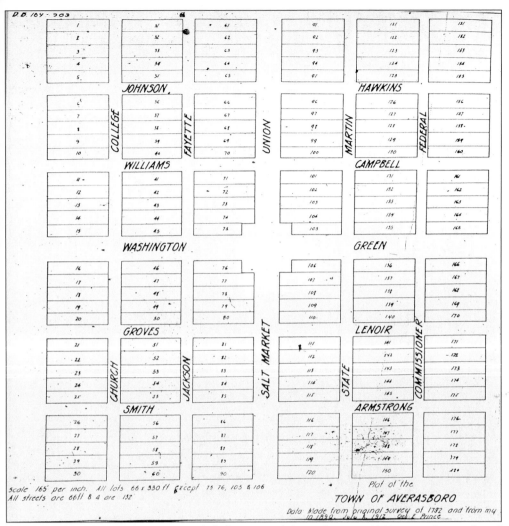

A 1912 Map. George Prince compiled this map of Averasboro in 1912 using data gathered from surveys in 1792 and 1890.

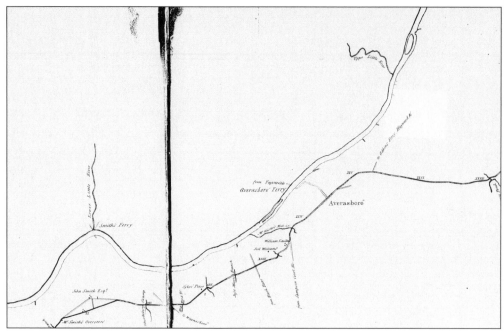

A PORTION OF BRAZIER'S MAP OF THE STAGE ROAD, 1818. This section shows the route of the road as it passed through the vicinity of present-day Erwin. (Courtesy N.C. Department of Archives and History.)

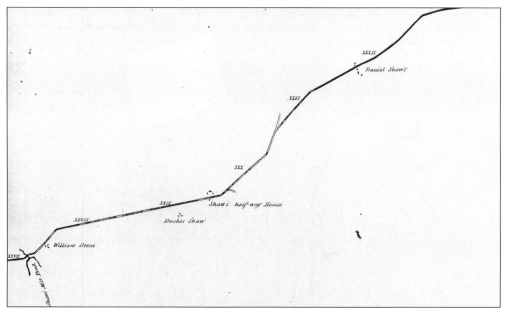

ANOTHER VIEW OF BRAZIER'S STAGE ROAD MAP. Here we can see the road as it passed through the present vicinity of Coats. Notice "Shaw's half-way House," which is still standing in 1996.

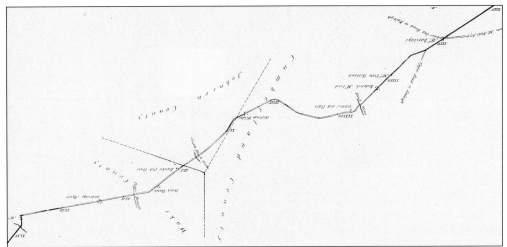

EARLY NORTHEAST HARNETT. Brazier's Stage Road Map also shows the route of this road as it traversed the northeastern portion of what is now Harnett. "Mrs. Barclay's" was the famed Barclaysville Inn.

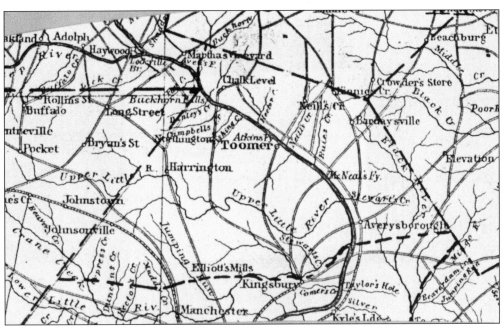

HARNETT COUNTY, AS DRAWN ON THE U.S. COAST SURVEY MAP OF 1865. The map was compiled in 1861, but publication was delayed by the American Civil War. Hence, the map contains information gathered in the 1850s, which explains why Toomer is shown as the county seat, even though Lillington became the county seat following a referendum in 1859. (Courtesy N.C. Department of Archives and History.)

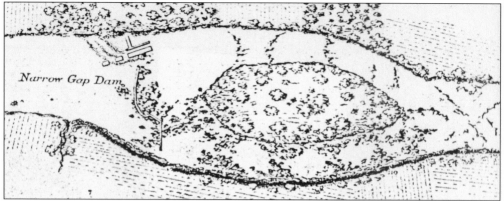

NARROW GAP ON THE CAPE FEAR RIVER NEAR ERWIN. This dangerous area was once feared by travelers along the river.

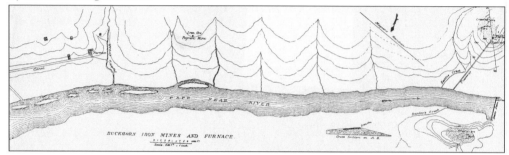

W.H. KERR'S MAP OF THE IRON OPERATIONS AT BUCKHORN, 1875.

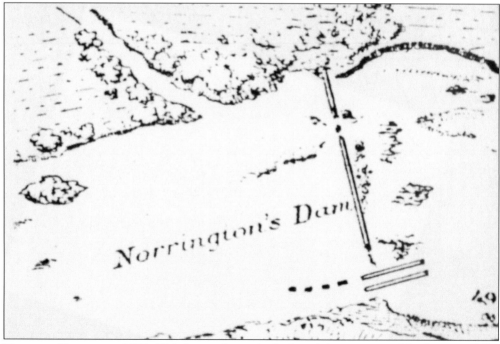

DIAGRAM DRAWN IN 1871. This image shows the lock and dam system at Northington Falls, now part of Raven Rock State Park.

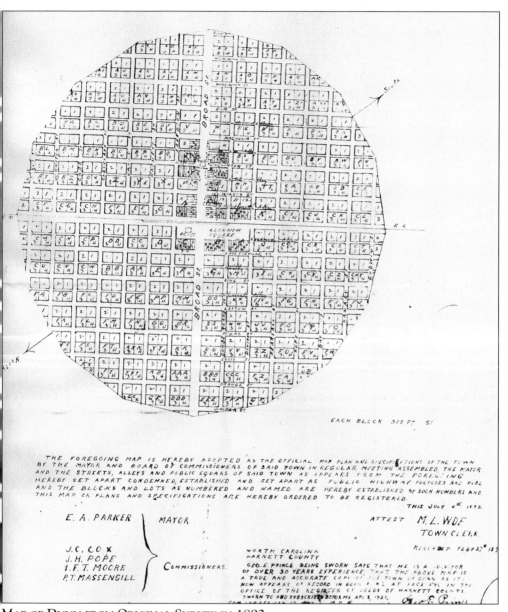

MAP OF DUNN FROM ORIGINAL SURVEY IN 1892.

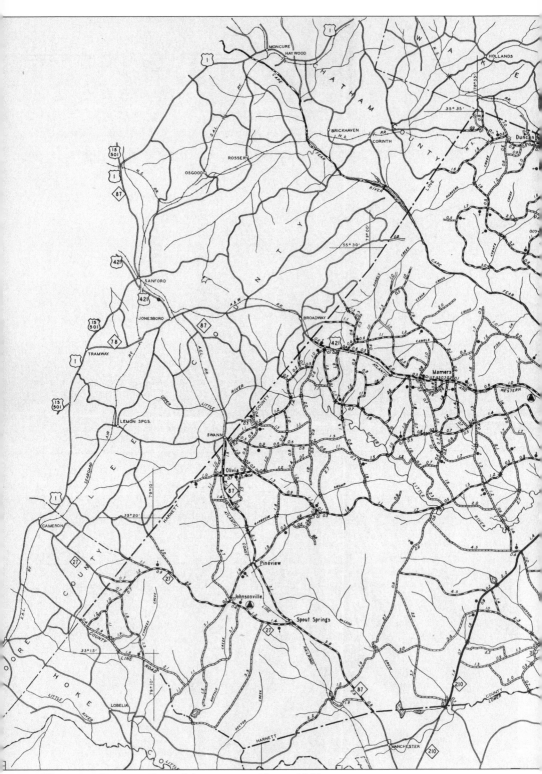

HARNETT COUNTY ROAD MAP FOR THE YEAR 1949.

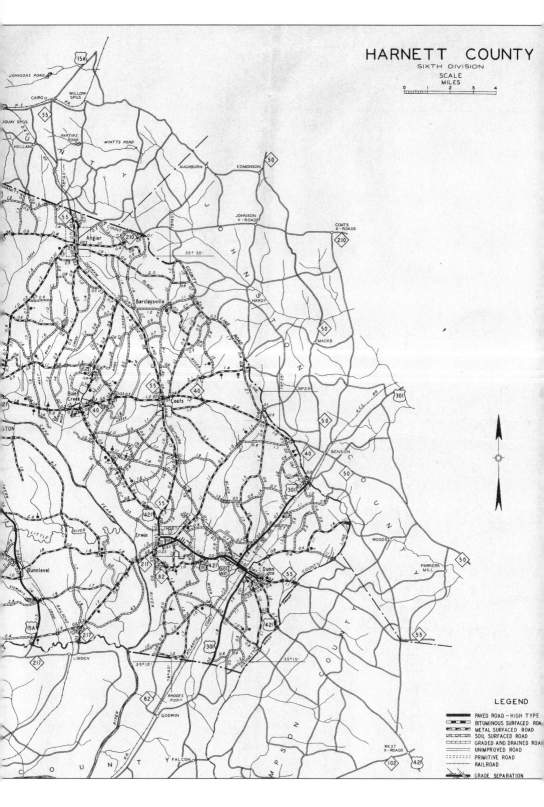

HARNETT COUNTY
SIXTH DIVISION
SCALE
MILES

LEGEND

PAVED ROAD — HIGH TYPE
BITUMINOUS SURFACED ROAD
METAL SURFACED ROAD
SOIL SURFACED ROAD
GRADED AND DRAINED ROAD
UNIMPROVED ROAD
PRIMITIVE ROAD
RAILROAD

GRADE SEPARATION

91

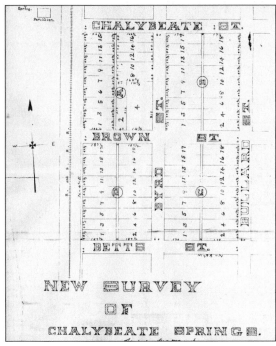

MAP OF CHALYBEATE SPRINGS, 1903.

MAP OF BUN LEVEL, C. 1920.

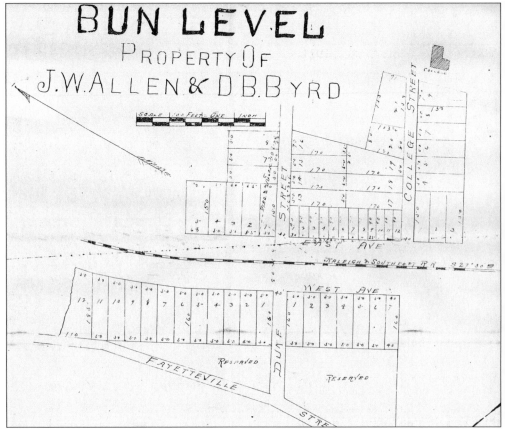

92

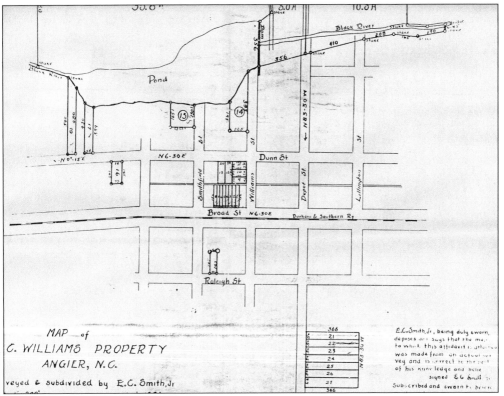

MAP OF DOWNTOWN ANGIER, 1921.

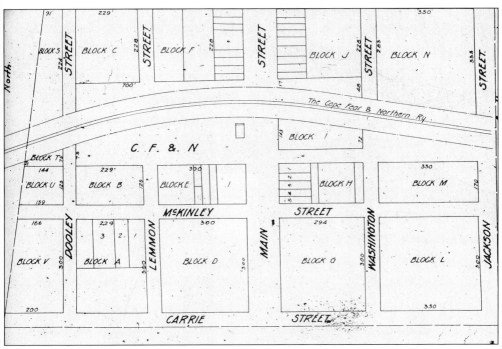

MAP OF COATS, DATED JANUARY 1, 1900.

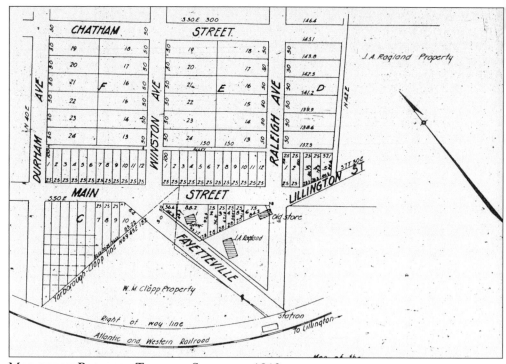

MAP OF THE PROPOSED TOWN AT SEMINOLE, 1913.

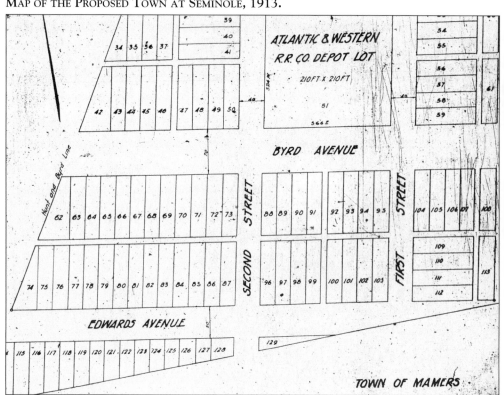

A MAP OF MAMERS.

A 1923 Map Showing the Settlement of Cambro. Cambro grew up around an extensive lumber operation along Anderson Creek.

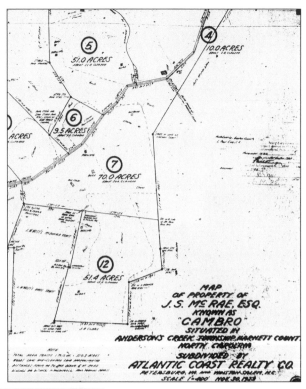

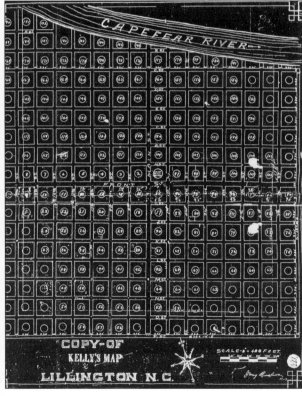

Kelly's Map of Lillington, 1907.

Acknowledgments

Several people helped in the preparation of this work, and they deserve special thanks. These individuals include Wanda Gregory, Vicki Brown, Starr Webb, Mary Cameron Byrd, Lois Byrd, Evelyn Byrd, and John Bethune. Steve Massengill, staff member of the North Carolina Department of Archives and History, was extremely helpful. Many of the photographs included here were the property of my grandmother, Dolly Strickland, who had a keen sense of history and kept alive many of the tales and traditions of Harnett County.

To everyone who lent a photograph or suggested an illustration, a hearty "thank you."

A PORTION OF THE 1896 POST ROUTES MAP OF NORTH CAROLINA. This section shows many of the small post offices across the county. Several of these locales no longer exist. (Courtesy National Archives.)